BORN WITHOUT A SILVER SPOON...

by

Angela Jacks

authorHOUSE®

AuthorHouse™ UK Ltd.
500 Avebury Boulevard
Central Milton Keynes, MK9 2BE
www.authorhouse.co.uk
Phone: 08001974150

First published by AuthorHouse   11/2/2007

ISBN: 978-1-4343-2586-0 (sc)

Printed in the United States of America
Bloomington, Indiana

This book is printed on acid-free paper.

Thank you to my husband, Mike, and my children, Michelle and Ben, that helped me and made it possible for me to write this story.

This book is based on true facts and events.

The story focuses on a boy's life, born during the Second World War and how his mother's circumstances effected his life. The story tells what happened to the boy, John, during his up bringing in institutes, and foster homes. The choices he made later on in his life that brought him face to face with Bolster, and jail and how he managed to turn every thing around to improve himself and become an honest, hard working man and a respected member of society.

CHAPTER ONE

During the Second World War, baby John was born.

Little did he know what lay ahead of him and the bumps on the road he had to face.

London was badly bombed by the German Nazi's and buildings and houses were destroyed. The landscape all around was dark grey and looked bleak – full of devastation and destruction. Dust was everywhere. It covered the capital like a big heavy blanket, big grey clouds hung in the sky, the weather was cold and unfriendly.

Londoners could taste the dust on their lips and see the heavy blanket around them like a cloak. The whole of England was suffering from food shortages, food rations were given to people, and people's lives were disrupted to take on their role in the war, be it manufacturing weaponry or assisting friends and neighbours in trying to continue their everyday lives as normal as possible. Overall, the situation looked bleak.

Jenny was eighteen years old, a tall slim girl with long blond straight and shiny hair.

Her pale skin accentuated her big blue eyes almost like aquamarine, fierce and shiny, her long legs were like they were curved to perfection. Jenny use to ware short skirts, and when she walked it seemed like she is floating gently. She was a stunning beauty and people used to stare at her when she walked.

Her sister Katy was four years older than her, she was chubby and short, with brown straight short hair and under her long dark eye lushes were a pair of shiny brown eyes.

It seems Jenny got most of the beauty between them.

They resembled each other in their facial features, but they had completely different colours.

Katy was very responsible and always looked after Jenny. They were very close, loved each other, cared and looked after each other.

After endless efforts to find a job in London, with no success, three months had gone by without any work they decided to look for a job elsewhere, they had to leave their mother in London, in a three cosy bedroom flat looking over the Thames.

Their search for work brought them to Derby. They were lucky to find a job in a big house as maids, like upstairs downstairs servants.

The house was a three-storey house, which has seven large, and beautifully decorated bedrooms.

They lived in the house, and shared a small room in the attic away from the family quarters.

The room was minimalist in style. They had two beds in the room, one in each corner, and a chest of drawers to share between them to store their clothes

The house belonged to a French family with four children who were rich and very upper- class.

The sisters' duties were cleaning, shopping and cooking, taking the two younger children to school and looking after them. The other two children were in their teens, and they worked with their father in the local pottery factory.

The French couple were in their mid forties and were very strict with Jenny and her sister Katy.

Jenny remembered the lady of the house, a big woman with two little black eyes, and very short black hair on her small head, two short fat legs supporting a big body.

She had a deep voice and used to scream at her in French 'rapido' hurry, hurry when Jenny was cleaning or cooking.

The family would throw the food at her when they did not like it and scream how stupid she was. They loved their food.

The husband and children were short and over weight. And appeared to be bouncing when they walked, and were very lazy. Jenny and Katy had to do every thing for them in the house.

The two sisters had Saturday and Sunday afternoons free from duties and they would go to the local pub and to the night club, to socialise.

About six months later, one Saturday night in April, the trees by the roads were in full bloom with all colours, pink, white, red, light blue and the sweet smell of perfume was hanging in the air, Jenny and Katy were dancing in the nightclub, having fun.

Jenny was suddenly aware of a young man staring at her. She looked up, he was a tall slim attractive young man with short, army cut style blond hair and piercing blue eyes. He walked smoothly and elegantly towards her introducing himself as Garry. He asked her to dance with him.

She was aware of her heart beating faster as they danced.

They danced until the small hours of the morning. His charm swept her, off her feet. She wished the evening would not end.

The next three months were like a dream for Jenny. She was so happy with Garry.

He was a soldier stationed at the local air base, and served as a gunman in the air force.

They met every weekend at the nightclub, dancing and laughing and having a good time. The weekends could not come quick enough so she could be with him.

One warm Saturday night in July, Garry asked her to marry him.

He explained that there was a possibility that he would be transferred to another base in Britain and soon would take part in the fighting in France.

"I don't want to lose you", he said, whispering with his lips pressed gently to her ear.

Jenny looked at him with her shiny blue eyes, she was all excited and said, in a teasing voice: "Let me think about it, it is a big decision". Garry's face expression was serious and gloom. He was waiting with a sense of fear of rejection.

The next few seconds dragged of long it felt to him like hours. Then Jenny laughed and said: O.k. I thought about it, Yes".

Garry's face lit up. He held her in his arms and gave her a big hug, kissing her face with passion.

The next day on Sunday afternoon, Jenny put on her best blue and white dress she kept for special occasions.

She looked beautiful, the blue in her dress accentuated her blue eyes. Garry wore his army uniform and looked very handsome. They got married in the registrar office and had a party in the local pub with few of their friends.

Jenny moved to live with Garry in his army rented accommodation house, but carried on working in the big house with the French family during the day.

The first six weeks went by like a dream, Jenny and Garry rushed home after their day work to be with each other.

Then one day Garry came home late at night, he was drunk and abusive.

Jenny was worried, and asked him: "What happened?" Garry started swearing at her, then mumbled some words she could not understand and he threw himself on the couch in the living room and fell asleep.

Jenny was waiting for him night after night. Until one day she decided to go with her sister and friends to the pub after work.

That night, when Jenny came home, Garry was waiting for her, they had a terrible row, Garry lost his temper, punching her, kicking her repeatedly when she fail on to the floor, shouting and screaming at her. "You will come home straight from work, do you hear me, you are not allowed to socialise with your friends after work, you are a married woman now". He left her on the floor bleeding, slamming the door behind him on his way out.

As she lay on the floor, mixed feelings washed over her, she was in shock, scared, afraid, and humiliated and in terrible physical pain. She couldn't believe that this charming man she loved with all her heart, could do such things to her. She laid there on the floor unable to move, thinking 'something was very wrong for Garry to do this to her, where all this rage came from, what has she done to trigger this kind of behaviour'.

A few hours went by. She helped herself from the floor, slowly making her way to the bathroom. She were standing under the shower, the running water helped soothe her injuries.

She stood there a long hour. Then slowly moved to the bedroom dressing herself with her nighty, her eye caught the time on the little brown clock that was standing on   her pink dressing table. It was four o'clock in the morning. She lay on her bed and fell asleep.

Her sleep was disturbed by horrible dreams, violent, shouting and screaming.

The alarm clock was buzzing. She woke up with a bitter test in her mouth.

She set in her bed and looked at the mirror across the room that was stuck on the big brown cupboard. She saw black circles around her eyes, her lips were swollen   and she had bruises all over her arms were she had tried to protect her head from the kicking feet of her husband. She was very sore and could barely move.

She decided to stay in bed and skip work that day. She was in to much pain and looked a mess.

Katy her sister was worried when Jenny did not show up for work at seven o'clock in the morning as usual. Jenny and Garry did not have a phone in their house.

Katy decided to walk to Jenny's house to check on her. It was a misty morning and it was raining, a fine nagging rain. Katy walked fast. It took her 20 minutes. She arrived breathless and wet, her brown short hair was wet and stuck to her head, drops of rain were running down her checks. She knocked on Jenny's door, and getting no answer, knocked again loudly. After ten minutes Jenny crawled to the door and opened it. Katy was frighten, "What happen to you?", she shouted. She helped her sister to her bed and put the kettle on the stove to make Tea.

With a cup of tea in her hand, Jenny told Katy what happened the previous night.

She was crying while she was talking. Katy was angry and upset. She made her sister's bed comfortable for her and said:" I have to go back to work, I will come later to check on you, and I will bring you some food, try to sleep, I will tell madam that you are sick".

Katy left to go back to work. She had to take the children to school. Mrs Blanch, the madam was angry at her:" what time do you say it is, the children won't have time for breakfast, they will be late for school". Katy tried to put a word in, but, it was no use,

Mrs Blanch was too upset.

Katy prepared a quick breakfast for the children and left with them to school.

That evening, Katy went back to Jenny with warm food to check on her.

Jenny was feeling better, she was moving about trying to tidy the house.

There was no sign of Garry, he did not come home that night.

The next day Jenny went to work as usual. She tried to keep her daily routine as normal as possible.

Garry came home that day in the evening with a bunch of flowers expecting Jenny to forgive him.

Jenny accepted the flowers with mixed feelings. She thought to herself 'I have to watch him from now on, how do I know when he is going to lose his temper again'.

All these thoughts went trough her head but she did not say anything to him.

They made up and things returned to normal. For a while Garry would come home straight after work and behave like a loving husband.

A couple a months went by. Garry started going to the pub again and returning home late drunk and abusive.

One night Jenny was waiting for him. When he walked in the living room, she was sitting there. "I have to talk to you Garry", she said. "What is it?", he answered.

"I am pregnant", she said. "What?", he reply, she repeated herself. He wasn't so happy about the news. "How's that happened?" he was mumbling. And than he walked into the bedroom and fell asleep on the bed.

Jenny sat in the living room for a long time, thinking what was going to happen to her and her baby.

During her pregnancy, Jenny continued to work in the big house. It was not easy on her but she carried on.

Two weeks before the baby was due, Garry came home and said that he was being transferred to France. "I hope it won't be long until the end of the war", he said to her.

Jenny was in tears, but said nothing.

CHAPTER TWO

On fifteen of April 1941, Jenny gave birth to a beautiful and healthy baby boy.

She and her sister were so happy. She sent a telegram to Garry by his base in Derby. In the telegram she wrote: 'You are now a father to a healthy baby boy, we are both in a good health, and I named the baby John'.

For the next few weeks she heard nothing from him.

She went back to work ten days after she gave birth, taking her baby with her to the big house.

Two weeks went by. The madam was not happy with the situation, she wanted Jenny's undivided attention.

So one warm morning at the end of April, the sun was shining and the birds were singing on the blooming trees, Jenny came to work with her baby as usual, she was happy and bright. The madam called her and said: "Jenny, I have to let you go, you are no good to me coming to work with your baby".

Jenny's face dropped, she was devastated, she couldn't say a word, tears were streaming down her face. She took her baby and left.

Katy carried on working and help her sister and the baby.

A year later the French family needed to go back to France to protect their interest against the advancing German army.

Katy and Jenny were left without any supporting means for their living and they decided to go back to London.

The three bedrooms flat in London was facing the Thames River, the place was warm and cosy. Jenny shared her room with her baby. Her mother and her sister helped her with John as much as they could.

Her mother loved baby John, and looked after him when the sisters were looking for jobs. They found day jobs, like cleaning, ironing clothes for other people.

Although food shortages were experienced all over the country, things hadn't seemed as bleak with her family around her.

Things finally hit rock bottom when London was bombed badly by the Nazi's Germans. Their home had been demolished, with it her mother and sister perished. Luckily, Jenny and baby John were in the 'Family clinic' for his routine check. Jenny was devastated when she returned home to find a pile of rubble and debris instead her home. She could not believe she lost her loved ones. She was confused and heart broken 'what she is going to do without her family, her mother and her sister Kate'. Big tears were streaming on her checks. She held her baby tied in her arms to comfort herself and to protect him. She was standing there among the crowd that gather around trying to help, staring at her home's ruing. Neighbours near by that escape the horrors took her to their home and tried hard to comfort her and offered her a shelter as long as she need it.

So horrible is a war. Many die both fighting for their beliefs and also by being at the wrong place at the wrong time.

A few days later a friend offered her the basement in Loughton.

Jenny moved with her baby John who was only eighteen month old, to a basement in a building in Birked Road in Loughton. This is the only place she could afford with a little money she had from odd jobs she did with her sister.

The basement was dark, wet, and cold, musty small was standing in the air, water dripped in through the damp walls and green yellow fungi was stuck on the walls.

Jenny did not find any work. She went every morning searching for work, but no luck.

Under these circumstances she was forced to prostitute for the little money which kept her and her son alive.

There was a large park with many trees near their home and Jenny an attractive young woman, tall, slim, blond hair with big blue shinny eyes would take clients there.

She hated doing it. She hated herself for doing it. But her son's life meant more to her. She would do anything she could to keep him alive.

John was left on his own all day, a baby in his cot, until his mother would return late at night to feed him.

One cloudy, cold and dark day in February, Jenny returned home earlier than usual.

It was around lunchtime. She ran for her baby, ran to get back to him so that he would not be alone. When she got to their dingy room in the basement, John was not there. Her baby, her two years old baby, was gone. Jenny was frantic with panic. She ran out of the basement, screaming for her boy, for her son.

Nearby neighbours heard her screams and ran to her. Jenny could hardly talk through her tears and anguish. "Where's my boy?" she gasped for air, trying to talk through her tears and terror. Her neighbour, a young girl in her teens who's clothes always looked filthy and her hair matted, said to her that the department of Social Services had come and taken him. "Where?" Jenny was frantic "Where?" "WHERE?"

But no one knew, not the girl with the matted hair, nor did any of the other people who had gathered around Jenny, attracted to her by her screams.

Jenny turned sharply and ran. She ran up the street, screaming if anyone had seen her baby, onlookers thought she was mad, not knowing who she was or what she was screaming about.

Jenny ran and ran. After some time of hysteria and anguish, time which Jenny had not been aware of, she found herself at the Social Services Offices. She barged in and scrammed "Where is my Baby?" A social worker, known only as Mary, from the name badge on her blouse, tried to calm her down. "Take a deep breath" the middle aged woman, with a kind face instructed her. "Take a deep breath and tell me what baby you are talking about". Jenny explained that when she returned home John was not in his cot – nor was he anywhere in their room. Mary held Jenny's hand in hers and gave it a light squeeze as she said, "Right, well, lets see what we can find out". After a few minutes, which seemed like endless hours to Jenny, Mary returned and with a factual tone in her voice said. "If we are talking about John Jones, two year old baby boy, then yes, he is in our custody and we have placed him at Peresbrook children's home…"

Jenny was frantic again, "Where is this place, I want my baby". "Listen to me" said Mary interrupting Jenny's hysteria, "we found his living accommodation unbearable and unacceptable. We had to do something for his survival".

Jenny was silent for a few seconds and than she said: "How did you find my baby? Is one of the neighbours reported to you?"

"No" said Mary and carried on "The police was chasing a deserted soldier in your building, and they heard a baby cry coming from the basement, and

they found John on his own, hungry and cold, and we came alone and took him to the children's home". Jenny carried on and asked Mary: "Are you going to ship him to Australia?". Jenny could visualize her son being taken away on a large ship to another continent.

"Oh no, he is too young" replied Mary.

During the war, children in their early to late teens were sent to Australia to live with foster families or to children's homes for their safety. Away from Europe and the War. Preparations for the journey were very difficult on the child.

Tonsils would be removed to prevent infections, colds and sore throats. Due to The war and minimal medical supplies, most being sent to the fighting soldiers, These operations would be performed with little or no anaesthetic, to the horror Of the child who not only suffered physically but also mentally and emotionally After being separated from their families.

Once she had managed to compose herself, Jenny demanded to see her son immediately.

That evening, the clouds hung low and the air was clammy, but Jenny and Mary made their way to the children's home to see John.

Mary's rusty white ford was one of a few cars still used by the public as most were used for the war effort.

Throughout the entire journey Mary spoke with a calm tone of voice to Jenny telling her "When you sort yourself out, and you could provide better living conditions for you and your son, you can get your boy back".

Jenny seemed to calm down a bit, and with tears running from her big blue eyes she nodded. Her full, short, blond hair swaying with the movement of her head as she agreed with Mary.

It was around ten o'clock at night when they arrived to the orphanage. Matron, a big heavy woman in her late forties wearing a grey stained white uniform welcomed the women. Her short black hair stuck to her head with grease and her round red sweaty face showed no sign of emotion. With a hard, dry voice she said: "It is very late to visit your child". Mary explained the situation and pleaded with her to let them see the baby. "No", said Matron, "Come back tomorrow morning". Mary comforted Jenny, while two muscled male workers from the institute kindly but firmly removed them from the premises.

That night, Jenny couldn't sleep. In the dark wet basement she listen to the noise of the night and to the dripping of the rain leaking into the basement.

In the early hours of the morning she finally managed to fall asleep from exhaustion. She was dreaming about her dead mother and sister. They were comforting her and wishing her a better life with her baby. Than she was dreaming about baby John, feelings of regrets washed her, may be she didn't do all she could to look after him. She was crying in her dreams and was very upset, she felt feelings of despair and helplessness.

Loud knocks on the basement door woke her from her disturbed sleep.

Once she woke up, she remembered her baby. She looked at the baby cot. The cot was empty, a sudden flash of her baby's memory went through her mind and she remembered Mary. She jumped at the door.

Mary's puffy and red eyes indicated that she too, had not had a very good night sleep. "It is time to go and see your son" said Mary as she turned and walked towards the white rusty car to wait for her.

During the journey to the children's home they were very quiet and did not swap a word with each other. Each of them kept her thoughts to herself.

When the two women arrived to Peresbrook homes, the matron welcomed them, again with no emotion showing in her big round red face, and took them to a little room furnished with a couple of old blue grey sofas.

They both sat on the sofa and waited.

Jenny had difficulty breathing. It felt like hours to her, just sitting there waiting.

She remembered her 'waiting time' in the Social Services office, waiting for Mary to come back with some news. Now she was finally going to see her son, her boy.

The door opened and a pretty young woman, 'petit', brunette with narrow green eyes was standing there with little Johnny in her arms. Jenny ran towards them picking her baby in her arms, tears were streaming down her face. "My little Johnny", she whispered kissing him and cuddling him. Rose the institute worker and Mary the social worker left the room.

An hour later they came back. Rose the pretty worker step towards Jenny to take the baby from her arms, Jenny refused to let go, John started crying 'Mama,

Mama'. Rose, took the baby firmly and with a dry tone of voice said: "You can come and visit your son once a week on Tuesday at ten o'clock in the morning", and left with crying Johnny.

Jenny was devastated, flood of tears covered her face, crying without the capability of stopping. Mary was heart broken and tried very hard to comfort her. Hugging her and saying soft and comforting words in her ear.

CHAPTER THREE

Jenny visited her son precisely every week on Tuesday and stayed with her son for a couple of hours.

John cried every time when the visit ended and his mum had to leave.

He wanted to go with his mother so much that he could not stop crying for a long time after she already left.

She always promised her son that one day she will have him back and they will be together as a family again.

His mother was always on his mind. He was asking for her all the time. This situation made him very distractive and he irritated everybody around him including the children in the home and the stuff.

John was four years old when he was transferred to Tim Lood lodge at the same children's home. He remembered the long grey corridors with rooms each side of the corridor. The large bedrooms were furnished to a minimum, five beds of each side of the grey walls. There were no cabinets to store clothes. The children kept their little clothes and items they had under their beds. He also could visualize in his mind this tall blond curly hair woman with a red dress with white dotes and the big cream colour straw hat which he called mother coming to see him every week. He was looking forward to these visits.

His mum used to bring him sweets. And take him for an ice cream in the near by pub. But when she left Rose the worker snatched the sweets from his little hands and said: "You are a naughty boy, and do not deserve any sweets". John burst into tears and cry for hours, but no one seemed to hear his cry and no one would go and comfort the little boy.

The care and treatment in this institute was cold and cruel, the manager who run the home was an ex-military man and he tried to run the children's home as an army unit.

The next two years John was a rebellion child, he always cried for his mother.

The staff gave him extra choirs like scrubbing the dormitory floors, washing his roommates soaks to keep him busy.

One visiting day his mother told him that she met a man and he wanted to marry her and adopt him. She was all red cheeks and excited from the idea of being reunited with her son and being a family again. John in his six years old mind tried very hard to understand what she was talking about. When he realised she said 'being together again' he was so happy and asked his mother: "Mum can you take me now with you?". "No" said Jenny, "but I promise it will happen very soon and I come and take you with me".

After this visit John did not see his mother for a long time.

Maybe because of her new partner or maybe because the children's home staff decided against his mother's visits. They claimed that John seeing his mother upsets and disrupted him too much.

John could remember since age four. He remembered Rose the worker, short, short brunette hair and narrow green eyes, all the children were scared of her. She was tuff and showed no patients or companionate toward the children in her care. She was a vein woman and was busy looking at herself on the mirror that was hanging in the   long grey corridor wall. She held his head under the water in the bath tab every morning when he woke up all wet.

She tried to frighten him to stop wetting his bed.

John dreaded the 'wake up time' at six o'clock in the morning. He knew what was coming for him. His little body would shiver all over, frightened from the cold water in the bath, and the thought that he won't be able to breath for a few long seconds terrified him.

He believed that if he will stay awake all night he wouldn't wet his bed. But, it always happened. He would fall asleep in the early hours of the morning and wake up wet.

John was tired all the time because of lack of sleep and his bed-wetting worsen.

The ignorant worker Rose kept torturing him and drowning him in the bath.

Shouting and screaming at him: "This will teach you a lesson, not to wet the bed". He was dreading the moment he would have to face sister Rose. Her job was to clean him up and she seemed to have some enjoyment and fun frightening the little boy, and drowning him in the bath tab. He remembered standing in the queue to the bathroom waiting for his turn to be washed. He was so scared that standing there made him wet himself again. This drowning system which Rose believed will cure the child from wetting his bed, simply magnified the problem in the child's mind and made him very tired and disruptive due to his lack of sleep. Trying hard not to fall asleep, trying hard not to wet the bed. Obviously the treatment did not work.

John was hungry all the time. As a child he used to sneak in the middle of the night onto the kitchen when everyone was asleep, and steal a piece of bread. In the morning he was punished for it. The breadcrumbs gave him away leading to his bed.

John could not understand how he was caught. The staff did not feed him as a punishment, he would go hungry until dinner time.

John particularly remembered one afternoon at spring time in April, the sun was shinning and a sweet smell from the blossoms was hanging in the air. It was bright and warm, he was nine years old, and he was working in the garden with few other children weeding the grass. Sister Rose came out with a tray full of sliced bread with peanut butter "Come and get it" she was calling loudly, all the children included John ran fast toward Rose to get a slice of bread before all of it will gone. John ran and stumbled into a rusty wheelbarrow that stood in the middle of the garden. He cut his stomach badly, but it seems that John's hunger was so great that he kept running toward the food tray. When he reached the tray with his little hands he collapsed and fell on the garden lawn, loosing his conscience.

Rose being of deranged mind carried on with her job giving the peanut butter slices to the children while she saw from her standing position that John was still on the ground and did not get up.

She thought nothing of it and went back to the kitchen to put the empty tray on the table. A few minutes later two children ran inside with their dirty boots and started screaming for help. Rose was furious when she came out to check "What this noise is all about. What's going on?" She yelled at the children "Why you are here with dirty boots?" The children were all excited and pointed toward John, He was lying in a pool of blood in the corner of the lawn, not moving.

Rose got scared and started screaming for help. The two-security men and the Matron ran towards the garden.

Asked Rose "What is all the commotion about?".

Rose pointed at John, Quickly the two men carried John to the nunnery near by the children's home.

Two nuns prepared a room for an emergency operation. John had two big deep cuts across his stomach, he was bleeding badly, the nuns tried their hardest to stop the bleeding, and sew the cuts as quickly as they could. While the two security men from the home held John down. He was screaming in agony. Every stitch the nuns sewed in his stomach gave him unbearable pain. After a few minutes John lost his conscience.

He had more than twenty stitches done on him without anaesthetics.

They were short on everything after the war, especially medicines.

After the operation the nuns put him in a room in the Nunnery to recover.

A day and a half later John woke up, he found himself in a big room, the sun shined on the two big windows opposite his white bed. He did not know where he was and what happened, a nun walked in and said: "Oh, good afternoon, you are awake, I get you something to eat". She left and after a few minutes she came back with a tray, on it, a slice of bread, a bowl of porridge, and a glass of milk.

John tried to sit up in the bed but the pain he felt was horrible. The nun helped him, she put cushions behind his back. He could smell the fresh fragment of the soap she used. John tried to eat, but he couldn't. He started vomiting. The nun examined John and found that the wound in his stomach got infected badly, and John developed high and a sever fever.

The nuns had to tear the stitches off, clean the infected area and sew the wound again. John experienced unbearable pain and he cried quietly until he lost his conscience, his little body could not take the great pain.

Two days later his condition remained critical, he was hallucinating, and came in and out of conciseness.

After a few days his condition remained critical. He almost died.

The nuns had to take him to the hospital for a proper care. John stayed there for over a year until he recovered completely from his horrible ordeal.

He liked it there, the nurses spoilt him, and he was fed and looked after, the volunteers in the hospital visited him every day and brought him gifts, soft toys, colouring books, crayons, and sweets and chocolates. Rose was not there to take away from him his gifts.

He could listen to music, from an old buttered radio that one of the volunteers brought to John's room.

After his recovery he was taken back to 'Tim Lood Lodge' Peresbrook children home.

CHAPTER FOUR

His first attempt to run away from the children's home was when he was ten years old. This attempt leads to frequent similar behaviour. John was fascinated with the big city, especially at night. He loved the colourful lights that reflected on the Thames River from the big ships that ducked there over night. For an unknown reason to him he was attracted and pulled towards the Thames area. He admired the block of flats that were standing there near the river. When he felt cold and hungry he returned back to the home, every time on his returning he was punished.

The most popular punishment was not to feed him.

One Friday afternoon in May, the sun was shining and it was quit warm, John with a few of his mates were busy weeding the garden, which was one of their chores after school, Rose called for him. John stopped his work and went to the kitchen. Rose was standing there with her hands on her hips. "John" she said: "We found you a foster family, who will pick you up tomorrow morning for a trial period". John stared at her with his big blue eyes. He did not know how to react and express his feelings. At last he thought 'I am going to have a family'. He dreamt about family life for as long as he could remember.

He was only ten years old, but he felt much older. "Well, John what do you have to say". Rose's voice was pushy and short. John looked at her and said:

"I will be ready Thank you, Ms". He was then dismissed to go back to his work in the garden.

That night John couldn't sleep, he was dreaming of what family life would be.

He saw in his dream a figure of a father, a mother and himself sitting around a Table. The table was loaded with food. He could almost smell and taste the roast pork and the baked potatoes, and his fostering parents kept asking him to help himself to more food. His mouth was watery and started to dript on his chin in his sleep.

He had a good feeling that someone cared for him.

It was early morning before he fell onto a deep sleep. At six o'clock Rose was calling to wake up. John was very tired, for a minute he lost track of where he was. Luckily that night John did not wet his bed. He gathered the few possessions he had such as; a little plastic comb, a tooth brush, a per of underwear, one shirt, a few marbles which he played with his friends at school, in a pillowcase and he was ready to face his new foster family.

At eight o'clock in the morning the foster couple arrived.

The couple, Mr and Mrs Hewitt's, introduced themselves to John. They were in their mid thirties. The woman was fat and cuddly and expecting a baby. The husband was tall and slim. Dark hair with bites of white hair showing on both sides of his head.

She hugged John, a nice whiff of lavender smell reached him, and she said what a lovely boy he is. Mr Hewitt's was more reserved, and shook John's hand.

After a long drive in the Hewitt's battered dark brown Volvo estate, they arrived at a block of council flats in Layton, London.

The couple had another child Charlie at home, a bit younger than John. Charlie showed John the three bedroom flat on the second floor John had to share Charlie's room. The second bedroom was a nursery for the expected baby. And the third bedroom was the Hewitt's. Mr and Mrs Hewitt's where very nice and warm towards John. They gave him a glass of milk and chocolate chip cookies in the kitchen after he put his belongings in Charlie's bedroom.

After a while Mr Hewitt's left to work and Mrs Hewitt's retired to her room to rest after telling John and her son to play together quietly.

The next day on Sunday Mr Hewitt took John and Charlie to the near by park. The children played football with Mr Hewitt on the grass and had a lot of fun. Mrs Hewitt stayed at home and cooked a Sunday roast.

When they came back, John smelled the pork roast, he remembered his dream, his mouth was watery and he was very hungry. After they washed and changed their cloths, they set around the table, his dream came true, on the table was the pork roast sliced thin in a serving big plate decorated with blue flowers on its rims.

The roast potatoes were displayed on a big deep white serving plate and the variety of vegetables, carrots, peas, and cabbage on the third white serving dish. The gravy was in a blue small dish and has it happened in his dream Mr and Mrs Hewitt's asked him to help himself and have more food.

After the meal they all retired and John and Charlie watched TV in the living room.

They watched their favourite cartoons.

The next day Monday morning the Hewitt's ask John if he was ready to go back to Tim Lood Lodge in Wanted east London. John was heart-broken, "What did I do?" he asked. "Nothing" they reply. "So why I am going back to the children's home". "We thought you knew that you will be with us only on holidays and some weekends" they said. John did not know about this arrangement. Rose did not explain this to him. "We just brought you to our home to see if you like it, and we will pick you up on Easter holiday to stay with us". Mrs Hewitt's carried on explaining. She was a kind lady, who suffered from ill health. She had only one lung and was straggling carrying her baby and needed plenty of rest.

John went back to the children's home and looked forward to the Easter holidays. As a child it seems to him very far away. But, four weeks soon went by and as promised by the Hewitt's they came and picked him. John remembers having a lovely time with the family. They gave him the feeling that he was one of them. One of the family. He was excited when he learned that they are all going to spend a weekend at the seaside in Blackpool. John was friendly and kind with Charlie.

All the way to Blackpool, they sang songs in the car, talking and laughing. They stopped on the motorway services once, and Mrs Hewitt bought them some sweets.

They arrived at midday to a B&B near the beach. The weather was comfortable, the sun was warm and a very light breeze was coming from the ocean. The ocean was blue, calm and inviting, few people were on the beach, running, laying on the send trying to catch a few moments in the sun. Children were playing with a spade and bucket digging in the white soft send.

They left their belonging in the room, Charlie pleaded with his parents to go straight to the beach. Being kind as they were, Mr and Mrs Hewitt's agreed.

They all walked to the beach, John and Charlie took their shirts off and run to the water in their shorts. The water was cold, they screamed in enjoyment and ran back to the beach laughing and joking. Mrs Hewitt gave them plastic spades and buckets and they were busy building send castles. Mr Hewitt went and bought ice cream for all the family.

John had happy memories from this trip to the seaside. He also spent summer holidays with them. He looked forward for the holidays, just to be with the Hewitt's, to have these feelings of belonging and be loved by a family.

After a couple of years the Hewitt's stopped coming to collect him for holidays.

John felt rejected again. He did not know what he done now. Rose did not bother to explain the situation to him.

Only after many years John found out what happened to the Hewitt's. They moved to Surrey, and Mr Hewitt's opened an Agency and Confectory shop. Mrs Hewitt's died a few years later leaving two children. Charlie was sixteen and his sister was eleven.

John was sad about the misfortune of his first fostered family experience. He loved the Hewitt's family who made him very welcome and happy when he spent time with them.

CHAPTER FIVE

When John was twelve years old he was sent to Surry to Brother Peter's children's home for the summer holidays. After a while John had unease feelings towards brother Peter. He saw how the brother put young children on his lap.

At night John heard loud crying. Some times, John got out of his bed and wondered in the long grey corridor hearing the crying, but he couldn't understand where it was coming from. John did not like it there and was happy when the holiday finished and he was allowed to return back to Peresbrook home.

John being a talented and gifted boy with a very high IQ, had behaviour problems and he irritated almost everyone around him, adults and children, because most of the time he felt board.

One summer holiday Brother Peter was addition for the church quire. He discovered John's voice. His voice was soft and strong at the same time and was very pleasant.

At first John refused to join the church quire, he thought it is not manly enough for him. In these days they used to call boys who engaged with creative activities such as: music, drama, art as sissy, but after a lot of persuasions, promises, and treats from brother Peter, John joined the quire.

His voice attracted more people to the church on Sundays and the donations were pouring in to the church box.

John decided to pay himself for his singing from the church's donations, and developed a plan to steal from the donation's box. He was very quick with his fingers. When he put a nickel into the tray he picked up a few nickels in his palm of his hand and put them in his pocket. With this little extra money, he bought sweets to top up his little food he got in the children's home.

At the time John reached sixteen a family in Essex, fostered him.

He turned to a very handsome young man, tall, wide shoulders, blond hair with big blue eyes.

He had good times with his second foster family. The family lived in a semi-detached house, three-bedroom with a big nice garden facing south.

The father was short and tubby. He had short grey hair. He was religious, Roman Catholic and all the family used to go to church every Sunday morning.

During the week he was working in the factory assembling carton boxes.

The mother was slim and short with short blond hair. Joan was a nurse and she worked in the hospital.

They had a fifteen years old daughter, slim and petit with big blue eyes and long blond hair, which John adored.

John had a sense of belonging to this family. May be because they resembled to each other by appearances.

The foster family had a friend called Robert who liked to hunt rabbits in the surrounding farms and he offered to take John with him on weekend hunting's.

John was very happy. Hunting and using the air rifle interested him. John and Robert soon became close friends. They spent Sunday mornings hunting.

Robert, who was a tall dark man on his late thirties, would pick up John to go hunting.

During the hunt, Robert would share a sandwich and a beer with John. They talked and laughed and had a very good time together.

They always came back with their prey, of around two-three rabbits and Joan used to cook Sunday lunch and invite Robert and his wife for a Sunday meal.

During the mealtime John and Robert would tell how they managed to hunt and catch the rabbets.

Robert's wife was a blond tall slim girt in her early thirties and she always used to stare at John. John felt embarrassed and did not say a word to her. He felt his blood rushing to his face when she was looking at him with her big green eyes and his heart would beat faster and faster. He always tried to avoid her. He felt that she wanted something from him, and she was sending him hidden massages with her body language.

She used to drop her handkerchief near her legs and asked John in her sweet voice: "Be a dear, can you pick up my handkerchief for me".

John moved slow towards the white handkerchief and pick it up, glancing a quick look at her beautiful crossed leg under the table. John blushing from embarrassment handed her, her handkerchief.

CHAPTER SIX

One sunny glorious Sunday morning in May, Robert' wife phoned and told John that her husband was waiting for him to come to their house and go hunting with him. John was all excited and said he will be there shortly. John did not stop to think why Robert did not come to pick him up as usual.

The couple lived a few blocks away from his foster family. John left the house running to Robert's house. When he arrived to their home, Robert was not there, his wife was dressed in a red silk gown showing her beautiful legs while walking towards John, her perfume smelled Roses, his mother used to smell like it. She started making suggestions toward John. John adored her because she was blond.

He liked blond hair women, they reminded him of his mother. He always missed his mother, although he couldn't remember her face clearly, he remembered her blond hair and her blue eyes, and her perfume's smell.

John got all excited and was about to kiss her, when Robert walked into the living room. Robert was furious, and John was frightened, John grabbed a rifle that was hanging on the wall. He fired twice without aiming at anyone. Luckily no-one got hurt but Robert called the police which took John to the police station and interrogated him in a small dark room without windows, a big mirror was stuck on the wall, so other detectives could see and hear what's going on. John was interrogated for hours without his foster parents to be present.

John was very tired and frightened. They accused him of planning to kill Mr Robert.

John kept repeating himself saying: "I did not plan anything, I fired the rifle because I panicked and I was scared". All of John's efforts to try and convince the police officers to believe him did not help. He was so tired and believed that if he signed the statement stating that he planed to kill Mr Robert he will be allowed to go home. John signed the statement, which incriminated him.

The police officers locked him up in the station's cell with a single bench on the side wall for sleeping accommodation and said: "In the morning we are going to notify your foster parents and you will be taken in front of the magistrate court".

John was very tired, but he could not sleep, bizarre thoughts flashed into his mind, he was worried what is going to happen now, he was worried about his foster family, 'may be they will reject me now, what is going to happen to me'. At the early hours of the morning he fell asleep. He dreamed about his mother, he was wondering in his dream asking himself 'where is she, why she is not coming anymore to see him'.

He suddenly woke up, he looked at his watch, it was six o'clock.

At first he did not know where he was, a bad feeling started streaming from the centre of his body all over. "Where am I", he thought. Suddenly he remembered, and the fear and tiredness he felt before crept all over him again. He waited, feeling very scared and very alone.

A few hours later around nine o'clock the police let his foster parents to see him.

They waited in the waiting room for over two hours. John was so happy to see them. He burst into tears and said: "It was not my fault, Jennifer invited me to her house saying Robert was waiting for me to go hunting". His foster parents looked upon him with lots of sympathy in their eyes, they believed him.

They knew Jennifer liked to tease men.

Bill, his foster father said to him: "do not worry too much, I am sure we can sort something out". His foster mother Joan was very quiet, and a helpless expression crept across her face.

They sat quietly barely looking at each other. Thinking different thoughts. Joan was praying for her fostered son. She grew attached to him and it was hard on her to even think that he was going to be taken away from her. The policeman appeared and said: "John confessed last night. He admitted planning to kill Mr Robert".

Joan was devastated, listening to the policeman accusations.

Later that afternoon John was brought in front of a judge who determined John's future. John was found guilty and was sent for two years to Borstal in Portland Bill in the south coast of Britain, which was a young offenders institute.

Chapter Seven

Portland bill was built on a rock in the island. The place had a history of war's prison.

Two hundred years ago it was built in Napoleon's time and the British used it as a prison for captured French soldiers.

Bill and Joan were tearful, and Joan gave John a big hug. The policeman had to tear John from her arms. He felt alone again and scared.

John and his foster parents waited in the back room of the courthouse, until they finish to trail another five cases, they were under the age of eighteen, the charges were of crimes such as car theft, sweet-shop robbery, and so on.

After all the trials finished, two policemen took all the youngsters to a police Van.

It was late at night, cold and pitch black in May, after a long drive in the policeman's Van.

They arrived at the Borstal. The staff gave them an army uniform and boots and escorted them to the dormitory.

It was a cell on average six inch by eight inch wide with a single bed against the wall, a wooden corner cabinet, a Jug for washing the face with aluminium mage, piss pot, and a desk with a chair.

Every wall in the place was painted grey. John felt like he was back at the children's home. The similarities, regime and atmosphere were very much alike.

The only difference was the staff's faces and the army clothes and boots he had to wear from now on.

That night he went to sleep without any dinner. He was very hungry. He woke up in the middle of the night with his stomach rumbling. He heard loud crying coming from the corridors. John got up and went toward the door. The door was locked. He was surprised and scared. He did not realised yet that he was actually in Bolster. He went back to his bed but could not fall asleep. He was waiting for the morning, with many thoughts running through his young head.

He missed his foster family.

About five o'clock in the morning a bell rung, the morning wake up call. By five thirty, the thirty young boys ranging from age fifteen to eighteen were ready for breakfast which consisted of porridge, bread and tea.

After breakfast John was called to the office, On his way he noticed that the borstal consisted of four large blocks standing in straight lines facing each other.

There were called Barracks. The blocks were named, John's block was called "Maria", the others were called "Nelson", "Granville" and so on. Near the office was a shop. They called it "Tauck" shop. The young prisoners bought there tobacco, toothpaste, sweets, razorblade for shaving etc', with the money they earn from working there.

The main aim in the bolster was to self generate and be self sufficient by learning carpentry and build wooden furniture, making clothes and schooling for their education.

The office was small, its walls were grey colour, with a big deep brown colour table in the middle of it, with two heavy deep brown colour arm chairs each side of the table. The office smelled of tobacco and coffee. On the table was a black looking phone and John's file.

A middle age man with black-framed glasses on his nose set there. His chubby body filled the arm-chair he was sitting in. The officer had a deep low voice when he explained the rules and regulations of the prison.

John would study from nine o'clock after doing his chores, until four o'clock in the afternoon and then he would continue his chores or work for the house.

John had a few choices of subjects to learn and work. He could learn and work carpentry or electric's or brick laying as most of the young boys choose to do.

John was told that the most important thing was that he must obey the staff.

The young prisoners called the wardens 'Screw'.

Most of the staff was ex-military service people, so the regime was quite tough.

During the two years that John was there he experienced few fights with the boys. It was all about control and leadership and John had a strong personality and was very stubborn, probably due to his tough early childhood, which contributed to his persona. These fights lead to solitary confinement. John was left drained. Empty feelings surrounded his soul, He felt desperate and confused.

He started thinking that life is not worth living.

His foster family kept him going on living. They sent him letters every couple of days, cheering him with kind words, encouraging him to hold on. In one of the letters, his foster sister wrote: "It is only temporary, you will get out soon when you are eighteen". These letters and the visits of his fostered parents kept him from doing a desperate act.

John studied carpentry, he loved it, and he progress very well. He liked the warm feeling that the wood transferred to him through his hands. He liked to cut it and mould it into something useful, as tables and chairs. His first work was a small table, which John was very proud off. The staff put it in the common room.

That day John walked to the common room every few minutes to see his creation, with feelings of satisfaction and pride. He thought 'I did that, I built the table'.

During these two years, his foster parents visited him regularly every two weeks.

Some times they brought with them sweets and cookies which John was grateful for, because he was hungry all the time due to food shortages the menu was very poor. Porridge in the morning, Cabbage and potatoes lunchtime, and bread and jam for dinner. The hunger problem rose when he couldn't ask for more, there was barley enough food for all the boys.

Chapter Eight

John was eighteen years old when he was released from Borstal. He was looking for a job to be able to rebuild his life.

His foster mother Joan knew of a builder and she put a good word in for him.

John started working with him. The builder was a middle age man with a beer stomach on him and a jolly kind meaty face.

His first job was to make a wooden coffin. The builder told John to take measurement of the body. John went over to the dead body and could only stare at it. The corps had a strange tone of colour. John thought that it reminded him of a waxed figure.

The desist was already prepared by the undertaker to be in the open casket.

It was his first time he saw someone dead. He was frightened and the builder said to him laughing: "go on, he won't bite you". John looked at the builder and at the body with his big blue eyes full of fear.

The body was an elderly man, tall and slim. John was wondering in his mind what kind of a life did he live'. After controlling his fears he measured the body and with the other two young workers that worked with the builder, they started cutting the wood and assembled the coffin. That day late afternoon they finished it.

They took a coffee break. John played a mischief and got into the coffin to have a feel of it. The two young workers notice it and shut the lid on him. He got scared and claustrophobic. After they had their laugh they open the lid, John was angry, very angry. It took him a long time to calm down.

John turned to be a hardworking young man and was happy and willing to do any job the builder asked him too.

He had a talent of making the work he was doing look easy and fun.

He was a quick learner, especially he loved every job in woodwork, painting and decorating. He had a good taste in choosing decorating materials for the builder's clients and everyone was very impressed and pleased with him.

One night John was on his way to meet his friends in the local pub. He walked in, and his eyes captured a young women laughing with her girlfriends. She was pretty with short shiny dark brown hair and a big brown green eyes. John was staring at her, his friends were talking to him. but he could not hear them. He was captured by her appearance and her laughter. A warm feelings spread down his loins.

Few minutes later he had the courage to introduce himself to her. "My name is John, can I buy you a drink", he blushed while he talked to her, but the dimmed lights in the pub did not give him away. She looked at him and smiled, "My name is Bridget", she replied "yes, I'd be delighted to have a drink with you".

John was over the moon. He signalled to his friends to leave him alone. She did the same with her friends and they found themselves sitting together with their drinks. She had a glass of white wine, and he had a beer.

They kept staring at each other. John with his fantastic big blue eyes, and Bridget with her lovely big brown green eyes.

Most of the time they were sitting quietly examining each other. He was thinking 'How great she looked and how sweet she laughs'.

She was thinking 'How great and strong he looks'. Suddenly they heard an urgent voice pleading with the Customers to finish their drinks, it is closing time.

Bridget looked at John and said: "Would you walk with me home, I live near by". John was very excited, "Yes" he said almost shouting his answer. They said their goodbyes to their friends and left. Bridget took him to a block of council flats. My flat is on the second floor she gasp quietly, "Would you like to come up and have a night cup", "Yes" he said holding her hand feeling the warmth of it. He was thinking, 'It might be my lucky night'.

She put the key in the door. John was stroking her shoulders. They walked together into the flat, and with great excitement and passionate they kissed each other, stroking each other and walked to her living room.

An elderly woman was sleeping on the couch.

Bridget waked her up. "You can go now". She said. The woman stared at them and said: "See you next time", and left.

Bridget looked at John and said: "She is my neighbour from the first floor".

John couldn't take his hands of Bridget and it seemed like he didn't hear what she said.

John pulled her straight into the couch. They made a passionate love and fell asleep together.

John woke up at five o'clock, a baby was crying in the background. 'Who is crying' he thought half asleep half awake. He crawled to the bathroom and splashed cold water on his face. Then he went to the kitchen, he saw Bridget holding a baby in her arms. The expression on his face was of a complete surprise, his mouth opened and he gasped for air and talked at the same time: "Who is this baby". "Is my baby?" said Bridget and add up "I have two children from a prior marriage. My husband left us six month ago. I have a daughter who just turned three years old and my son is eighteen month old". John stared at her and her baby and then said: "I have to go to work now, I'll speak to you later". And he left.

By the evening John missed Bridget very much, even the responsibility of two young children did not frighten him away. His feelings were very strong towards her and he had a soft spot for children, may be because of his up bringing in the children's home.

That day in the evening he phoned her, and she invited him to her flat for dinner.

During dinner, she told John about her ex-married life, and how every thing went wrong when her ex-husband was made redundant from the Metal factory. They experienced hardship and financial difficulties they faced day after day ruing their relationship and one thing lead to another. Her ex-husband became violent and started biting her. This situation lasted for over a year and she decided to do something about it, and got divorced. Her ex-husband's parents helped. His parents loved the children and helped her with them anyway they could. Although she wanted badly to keep the family together, in her opinion it was not possible. The children were frightened all the time because of their loud arguments and the physical violence they witnessed.

John felt very sad for her, and he wanted to protect her, she looked so fragile.

For the next eight months they were together all the time in the evenings.

When John finished work, he went straight to her, he also started supporting her financially and he was happy to play with her two young children.

The baby boy was adorable, smiling al the time, his face light up when he saw John.

The little girl looked like her mother, dark hair with green eyes, she too liked him.

They spent most weekends at the park with the children playing ball and feeding the ducks and some evenings they spent at the local pub. Bridget's ex-husband barley came to visit his children. He got involve in a criminal activities which put him away in jail for a long time.

Time went by and one warm evening in the spring, John invited Bridget to dinner at his place, a rented accommodation, one bedroom unit. When he served the desert he pulled out of his pocket a little box, knelt on one knee and asked her to marry him,

Bridget blushed, her green brown eyes sparkled when she looked at the diamond ring, she said: "Yes" with her little voice. Both of them were excited, they kissed each other, stroked each other and they found themselves on the dining room floor.

After a couple of hours John took Bridget to her flat.

Three month later they got married in the register office and had a party with their friends in the back room, of the local pub.

CHAPTER NINE

Bridget suggested that John move to her flat and live together. He accepted.

John kept his job with the same builder.

Every morning at six o'clock, John put his tools on each side of his bike and rode to work, the tools dangled from side to side. He worked all day finishing late in the evenings. He worked hard every day.

Three month later John realised that the money he was earning was not enough to support his wife and his two children, John adopted the children and gave them his name. He started doing decorating jobs on weekends and late evenings after his day job. He was hardly at home, working hard, his first baby was on its way as well. John wanted to give everything his family required and more.

These thoughts kept him going.

After a while John bought himself an old white van for work. Because of his good reputation he had a lot of work and he had to carry many tools. He was so happy with his new second hand white van. He put all his time and energy into work. And obviously his roles as a husband and a father suffered.

Every day he left home for work very early in the morning and came back home late at night.

One day he came home earlier than usual and he did not find his children at home. Only Bridget was there cleaning the place. "Where are the children?" he asked Bridget. "They are at my ex-in laws house", (next door to them) she said. "Call them in" said John. Bridget said that the in-laws refused to let the children go home. They were very fond of the children and looked after them for Bridget.

They were an old couple in their seventies, very warm and kind to their grandchildren. They also felt guilty conscience because their son abounded his children. They tried their best to make it right.

They did not like John at all because of his hot temper, and because he was barley at home. John made a point to come home earlier than usual for the next week and every time the children were at their grandparents house. John did not like them, In fact he did not like many people, and was suspicious of them. Because of the cruel up bringing he had as a child. In his childhood many adults disappointed him and did not treat him right.

One cloudy day late afternoon, John went to Bridget parents in laws' house and demanded his children to go home with him. They refused to let them go.

John started shouting and swearing at them. The in laws got frightened and called the police for domestic disturbance.

Even the police officers seemed to be against John, and disagree with him on the decision to take his children home. John lost his temper with the police officers as well, and started shouting and swearing, offing and blinding, losing control of his language.

The children loved their father and their grand parents. They got very scared seeing the rows between them.

They felt torn apart and very much wanted to go home with John, but they were scared that their grand parents will not like them anymore and may not let them come back to their house again. The children stood there while the oldest girl held her little brother, crying quietly. No one seemed to pay any attention to the children in the heat of the big argument and the shouting and the swearing between the adults.

The two police officers arrested him in front of his children, Bridget's parents and the entire neighbourhood, who gathered around and watched.

John spent the night in the police station and the following morning he was released.

He went to work that day as usual. That night he did not go home, he went to the pub to meet his friends.

In the mean time Bridget was waiting for John. She was very much pregnant and she was waiting any day to give birth.

She was worried when the following day John did not come home again.

She started phoning his friends looking for him. They promised her that they would tell John that she is looking for him. On the third night John came home.

Bridget greeted him with screaming and shouting: "Where have you been? I was worried sick about you", John took her in his arms and held her, and he said nothing.

After a short while Bridget assorted herself and carried on with her chores. She put the children to bed and tucked them in. John kissed them goodnight.

John and Bridget had a quite dinner together. After dinner Bridget said: "I am ready to go to the hospital". John looked at her, and got panicked, she took the little bag she prepared earlier and was ready to go. John put himself together and drove her in his Van to the hospital.

That night Bridget gave birth to a healthy baby girl. Her giving birth was quick and relatively easy comparing with her other two children.

She was very happy about the new baby that she did not think about the financial side of it. John tried hard to be happy for her and said: "Do not worry my love, I'll work even harder to provide for us".

Bridget staid one day in the hospital and she was released the following day. John went to work and worked very hard, in the evening he went to a decorating job for one of his clients. He finished his job around nine o'clock and did not feel like going home. Instead he went to the pub to meet his friends and tell them the good news about his new baby girl.

Late that night he came home, he was drunk and felt ashamed of himself. Bridget told him off. He mumbled incoherent words.

All that week John came home late at night and he was quit drunk most of the time.

Bridget did not know what to do or how to handle the situation.

After a few weeks John got use to the idea of a new baby and he become himself again. He worked hard and came home straight after work.

After a while Bridget demanded more house keeping money from John, He did not have it. They started rowing every evening about money and they said nasty things to each other in the heat of the moment.

The atmosphere in the house was unbearable for a long long time.

Eighteen months later, one night in February, cold and dark, Bridget had good news for John, after their dinner she said: "I am pregnant again". John's face dropped, he was thinking about the financial strain that the new baby will add on him. He could not be happy like Bridget and he could not pretend anymore. These feelings cause him to resent his wife and he started going to the pub after work every night. He could not face Bridget's complaints about her condition on top of his financial worries.

It was hard on her being pregnant after eighteen months of the last baby girl. She was a Roman Catholic religious and she was not allowed by her religion to take birth control peels or use any other contraceptive methods.

One late night in November, Bridget woke up John, he could barely open his eyes, he got home very late that night. She started screaming at him "Wake up, I am ready to go to the hospital". John jumped and looked at her, she was all puffy and red around her nose. "What's happening to you" he said. Bridget could not stop screaming at him. "Take me to the hospital the baby is coming". John suddenly realised what she meant. "Oh, it is time" he mumbled. He helped Bridget to get up the bed, took the ready little suitcase that Bridget prepared a day before, and drove her to the hospital. She was in a lot of pain, she was screaming and blaming John for her pregnancy. It took her six hours of suffering until the baby came. John was escorted out of the room to the waiting room. Few minutes later a baby cry was hanging in the air. The nurse delivered the good news to John. "You have a healthy baby boy". John was ecstatic. "Can I see them?" he asked. "Yes, you can". John rushed into the labour room. Bridget was laying there all sweaty and red, but with a big smile on her face, holding a little baby rapt up with white lining. He came and held her hand, he got emotional, warm filings washed him and he shaded a few tears from his corner's eyes. Both of them were over joy and looked at each other with love.

John and Bridget were so happy. They forgot all the bad times they previously experienced.

Over the next few weeks John was again a loving and understanding husband.

He tried to help Bridget with the baby anyway he could, in between his jobs.

Eighteen months later, the arguments and fights between them started again and got worse. The main cause of the fights and arguments was money. It did not matter how hard John worked and the long hours he put in. it was not enough for Bridget. All these fights between Bridget and John made him feel inadequate and when he finished his working day he did not feel like going home. He started sitting in the pub every evening until closing time. The situation between Bridget and

John became unbearable.

One evening John was in the pub drinking with his friends.

John started feeling bored with his friend's conversation, about their financial problems. He ordered a round of drinks and started flirting with the barmaid.

She was quite jolly, a long blond hair, tall and chubby with big blue eyes,

She was pleasant and responsive. She laughed and joked with him.

John forgot for a moment his family's problems.

He asked her for her name. "Caroline" she said. "What are you doing after work?" "Nothing much, I live in the flat above the pub, if you want you can come up with me for a night cap" she said. John got all excited.

He waited for the pub's closing time. He was looking at her and he liked what he saw. Her long blond hair shone in the dim pub lights and her blue eyes Sparkled when she served drinks to the customers.

After closing time John helped Caroline to finish clear up around the pub and he joined her at her flat upstairs.

It was a self-contained bed-sit with a little kitchenette.

All the walls were painted Magnolia colour, and it felt good, light and airy.

She offered him a beer and they talked and laughed. They felt good together and they couldn't resist the physical attraction between them. John was in his late twenties and his hormonal system took over, She was in her early twenties. He stayed with her all night, early morning he went to work.

The big excitement between John and Caroline carried on for a week, every night he accompanied her to her flat.

John's friends gave him a massage from his wife to go home.

John had a feeling that Bridget wanted to tell him something important.

That night he went home. John and Bridget had a terrible row and in the heat of the moment she said to him: "I am pregnant again". The news felt like a slap across his face. The new baby was only fourteen months old.

John was very unhappy and angry to hear the news. He left slamming the door behind him. He went to Caroline, thinking to himself 'My God, how I can support my family, a family of five children with the new baby to come'. He was all confused and scared.

Hours later he found comfort in Caroline arms. She did not know that John was a married man. And she was falling in love with him. John spent a couple of weeks with her until he decided to go home to see his wife and his children. He tried hard to make peace with Bridget.

He also kept seeing Caroline on a regular bases. He had a very busy schedule with his work, family and a mistress. He lived a double life.

Chapter Ten

His wife gave birth to a healthy baby girl and once more John tried his hardest to please her. He went home straight after work, helped her with the daily chores in the house, such as; shopping, cleaning, looked after the children at night, bath them and fed them and put them to bed. He did not go near the pub. This good behaviour lasted a month. Than one night he went to the pub.

He met Caroline and she had good news for him. "What is it"? Asked John. "You will have to wait until we go to my place" said Caroline. When they reached her flat, John asked again: "What is it?" in his heart he knew the answer, but he was hopping he is wrong. "I am pregnant", said Caroline. John looked at her with his mouth open. "Are you sure?". He asked, breathing heavily. Caroline looked at him very surprised, she never saw him like this before and said: "What's the matter? I checked with my doctor last week, and yes I am pregnant". She kept on "Don't worry, I don't want to get married, not just yet". John's face lit up and his breathing settled to normal. Yet he didn't tell her that he was a married man with six children.

John was living with two women, none of whom knew about each other. He shared his time between his work, which was his first priority and then his women.

His financial situation worsened when the local constable caught him speeding.

The constable a tabby chap, warned him a few times previously to slow down his speed. But this time the constable insisted on giving him a speeding ticket. John lost it after his persuasions to avoid the ticket failed. He started shouting and swearing at the constable which led him to press charges against John. Few days later at the magistrate's court John's driving licence was taken away from him for the duration of three month and he got fined of two hundred pounds. It was very hard on him. He had to get back on his pushbike to continue his work.

His visits to the pub and Caroline's flat were rare and reduced to once a week.

John barely saw his children. They always seemed to be at their grand parents.

Bridget was very edgy and did not stop complaining to him. This last pregnancy was hard on her. Overall John's life looked very grim.

One warm night in April he went to the pub to meet his friends and one of them a scruffy looking, short fellow, with biddy black eyes, his greasy brown hair was stuck on his small head, and his big hears popped out of his head, he smelled of tobacco and beer. He came up with an idea to earn a lot of money. Whispering in John's ear, that 'friend' was saying: "There is this Metal factory worker I know, he can help us shift few tones of metal and I know a scrap yard man near by. He is willing to buy it from us "What do you say? Are you in?". John said: "Let me think about it, I'll let You know tomorrow night". "Don't leave it to long" said the 'friend'.

John went home, the flat he was living in with Bridget was over crowded with five children. He was laying on his bed unable to sleep thinking 'very soon I will have six children, It would be terrific if I can afford to buy a house for my family'. John thought about his 'friend's' offer. More he thought about it, More attractive it became. He thought to himself 'it looks easy enough if they have the support of the security man that worked there and have the knowledge of the ins and outs of the place'.

The following night John went to the pub. He met his 'friend' and said: "Ok. I am in". His friend said to him "Let me organised a meeting with the metal factory worker and another two of my mates". John did not know that more people were involved in it. But he felt that he gave his word and he could not go back. He decided to take a chance and go with the flow.

The next night they all met in the garden shed of the "inside job" man who was a tall, lanky man with big brown eyes on his narrow face, an innocent expression was on his face. His job at the factory was as a night security man. They all discussed the plan of attack.

He was willing to let John's van in, load the stuff and take it to the scrap-yard man.

They all agreed to do it the following night.

Chapter Eleven

They all worked hard that night and loaded a few tones of metal into John's van.

They unloaded the stuff at the scrap yardman's back garden. He promised to pay them as soon as he sell it on to some people he knew in London. John had bad feelings about the old scrap yard man and did not trust him, he looked slime, thin little old man with two little eyes closed to each other, greasy thin white hair stuck to his head. They all agreed to the payment deal and John went alone with it.

The others seemed to trust him.

A week went by and John hadn't recovered anything for his part of the robbery.

He talked to his 'friend' about it and they realised that everyone was waiting for the money.

Another two weeks went by and one late night John woke up by loud knocks on the flat door accompanied by shouts of "Police, open up". John hurried to the door wearing his blue gown over his pyjamas. He opened the door and asked the two police officers that stood there: "What is the meaning of all this noise at this time of the night, what's going on". During all the commotion the children woke up and started crying. Bridget went in to the children's room to calm them.

The police officer stood square on to John and said: "you'd better come with us to the police station. Have suspicion that might know about a recent robbery that took place at the metal factory". "What robbery, what metal factory?" asked John. "Come with us, and everything will be explained to you at the station",

Said the police officer. John got dressed and tried to comfort Bridget by saying, "do not worry, I will be back soon". He turned and left, walking out of the front door followed by the two police officers.

In the police station John looked through a glass door into an office where he saw the old grey haired scrap yard man talking to a police officer. John couldn't make it out what he was saying. Suddenly the scrap yardman looked over at him and pointed at him with his finger. John then knew that he was in a very deep trouble.

A long and tiring hour went by before John was called into the office.

The scarp yard man still standing there said in a loud and clear voice: "This is   the man who organised the robbery, and without my permission they dumped it   in my back garden. And a few days later the metal piles disappeared from my place".

John got so angry listening to his lies, he swung at him quickly before anyone could stop him. He punched the man on his face and scream at him: "Liar, Liar, burn in hell". Three police officers rushed into the office and restrained him.

They polled him into a cell still kicking and screaming. John was so frustrated,   he continued shouting and swearing., but no one acknowledged him, no one seemed to hear.

After a long while, John didn't know how long, but all the anger, hurt and betrayal died down and he was much quieter, a detective approached the cell door, John could hear his footsteps. He stopped at the door and spoke through the grill with a firm tone of voice "Are you ready to answer a few questions?"

John looked at him and said: "Yes". He was taken to the investigation room where two detectives joined him with a tape recorder.

They stated their names, date, and time. "Pc duck and Pc Harry are interviewing John Jones concerning the robbery that took place at the Mattel factory on fifteen of February this year".

During the investigation one of them played the good detective role while the other played the bad detective role.

John was angry and confused. He demanded a lawyer and said that he would say nothing until a lawyer was present. They couldn't refuse him, but they did not let him go home. They explained their entitlement to hold him in the cell for 24 hours without any charges.

John did not sleep much that night.

His thoughts were about his wife and his children, and about his mistress carrying his child. He couldn't believe how he got himself into this mess.

He kept thinking, and dreaming about his childhood. Only fifteen years ago he was in institutions such as the children's home and the Borstal. Pictures and scenes from his past kept running in front of his eyes. He also felt the pain that accompanied these scenes. Cold shivering feelings passed through him, when he saw in his mind again and again, how sister Rose kept drowning him in the bathtub. He also felt the pain in his stomach when he was so hungry and ran to pick the pinnate butter slice of bread from the tray and stumbled into the rusty old wheelbarrow that cut his Tommy. He heard loud voices, and long quite crying ripping his head, the type of noises he heard when he was in Borstal.

All his past feelings of fear, anger, uncertainty and confusion came back to him. He was very angry with himself. How could he have been so stupid?

The need for extra money to improve his family's life style took control of his senses and logical thinking.

John was an intelligent man. He knew he made a big mistake. He knew he was going to pay for his mistake with his freedom. The fear of not knowing exactly what was going to happen to him and his family now controlled him.

At nine o'clock the following morning, a police officer served John breakfast and told him to get ready for questioning with the state lawyer he was appointed. John couldn't eat breakfast, his stomach rumbled with tension and fear. He took a deep breath and said to the police officer "I am ready".

In the interrogation room the lawyer, a middle age man, tall, slim with spectacles on his nose, advised John not to say anything, and requested to be left alone with John.

John confessed to the lawyer about the plan to burgle the factory and how he and 'friends' moved twenty tones of copper with his white van from the metal factory to the scrap yard. The lawyer advised John to plead guilty so that he could cut a deal with the district attorney for him. John not knowing much about the law, accepted the lawyer's advice and was release on bail.

The court case was arranged very quickly. Three weeks later John and his 'mates' sat in the courtroom. John was very surprised and angry when his 'mates' pointed fingers at him declaring that he was the ring leader. The trial was conducted with no jury, only the judge sitting on a raised platform back to the middle of the wall in the Courtroom.

At the end of all the testimonies, the judge decided on the punishments. He sent John's 'mates' to jail for two years, and John was sent to jail for five years. The Judge declared that he believed John to have been the brains behind the operation, the leader, which of course, he was not.

Bridget was in court, and started screaming and crying after hearing the verdict.

John was in shock.

John was given a few minutes alone with his wife in a small room at the back of the court-room. He told her how much he loved her and he asked her to appeal for him to the high court. She was crying. The tears streamed down her cheeks.

That picture was engraved in John's mind and would often surface when he though of his family.

Two guards, both of whom were very large and stocky, took John with them to a police van outside. John was driven to prison in Surrey.

Chapter Twelve

Prison was a big dark colour building. Small windows with bars were spread equally on the top of the building walls, like black eyes of a big monster starring at a high wall. At the top of the wall, there was a fence with metal spikes, the wall surrounded the all prison's area.

Security tower were standing at the border of a big yard, where the prisoners had half an hour a day for a break from the prison walls. They walked there, excised, played ball or just sit in the fresh air.

They also used to conduct their business in the yard, such as: selling cigarettes, chocolates and sweets, little presents for their family.

Beside conducting business, some of the inmates settled their disputes and grievances by fighting. In a few occasions an inmate knifed their opponent.

The guards had to get involved to prevent serious injuries.

After he registered in the prison's office, he was allowed to have a shower, and then the staff gave him his prison uniform. The uniforms were grey in colour and brought strong memories about his childhood. His cell in prison looked and felt familiar.

The walls were painted grey and the smell was musty and unpleasant, he had to share the small cell with another inmate.

The other inmates seemed to be bigger and more threatening.

He had to get use to institution life again. It was hard on him, as he had had ten years of independence and freedom after his sentence in borstal.

The first couple of weeks in jail John were very upset. He did not talk or responded to anyone, inmates or wardens. He was very quite and kept himself to himself.

The prison management decided to send him to work in the carpentry workshop.

John worked hard to try and forget where he was.

He was very aggressive towards the inmates and they finally left him alone after a few physical disagreements.

John waited for his appeal. When Bridget visited him on a cold January day, she delivered John the bad news he dreaded…his appeal was denied.

This made John very frustrated.

During his shower entitlement that day, John had another disagreement with another inmate.

Murderous Matues as they all called him, he was a big fat and tall fellow with a baby face. He was inside for life on a murder charge. He murdered his wife because he suspected her on cheating with another man.

Both of them were strong and stubborn – wanted to show they were muscular and man.

It resulted in both men being taken to the prison infirmary.

John was kept in there for five days.

When he was taken back to his cell he found an interest of making things. He was a gifted painter and started making greeting cards.

In no time at all John's work was verbally publicised by the inmates and they started ordering greeting cards for their families. Birthday cards, Get well soon cards, Thank you cards etc'.

John gained the trust and respect from the inmates and the prison's workers.

They admired his skills and talent.

John was making money to buy cigarettes, and materials for his work. But most of it he gave to his wife during her visits.

He also used this opportunity being locked in to study an engineering course by post through 'City and Gilds".

He was studying every night under his bed cover with a torch until the small hours of the morning.

Lights out in prison was at ten o'clock at night.

John was very busy.

During the day he worked in the carpentry workshop. Late afternoon he made greeting cards and wooden toys in his cell and during the night he studied. He made sure that time will go quickly and he will be out of Jail in no time.

One year into his sentence the prison warden grew fond of him and gave him errands to run for him outside prison. As John was in prison on a 'Minor' charge this was possible.

This gave him a sense of freedom for a few hours a week, which boosted his moral.

He used to drive the warden's car to get the warden's children from school occasionally, and some times to collect dry-cleaning. John never failed the Warden expectations. He was loyal and trusted.

Until one day the warden asked John to go and collect the inmate's wages. John collected them from the council offices.

On his way to the prison John opened his little brown envelope, which contain his wages and bought himself ten cigarettes. On his arrival, John gave the warden the car's key and the inmates little wage brown envelopes.

The warden saw John's wages envelope opened and he said to John: "What happened to your wage's envelope". John said: "I bought some cigarettes on my way back". The warden hit the roof. He was angry and said: "You know you are not allowed to use your wages until it is giving to you by me. Now I am taking all your privileges from you. No more running errand's for me, you are going to stay in the prison area".

John was shocked from the warden's outburst. He looked at him and said nothing. John was dismissed. He went back to his cell, still do not understanding what he had done wrong to triggered the warden's outburst.

John had lost the little freedom he had when he was running errands.

He decided to finish his sentence quietly, concentrating on his work and studies.

His work had a great demand. The guards and the warden ordered wooden beds, for their children from John, supplying him with materials and paying him some money for it. His wooden toys had also a great reputation and everyone in the prison ordered a wooden toy from him, like little wooden cars, tracks, trains, and so on for their children.

His wife visited him every two weeks on a regular basis.

When John had been in prison for about three years, one hot and sticky visiting day in July, Bridget burst in to tears. They were streaming on her red and sweaty face, mixing with her sweat, and said to John that she filed for a divorce and she was not going to visit him again. John was very sad. But he said nothing. The following day he asked the warden to grant visiting permit to his mistress

Caroline. She started seeing John once every two weeks. She told John that he is a father of twins. Boy, and a girl. John was very sad not to be able to see them

CHAPTER THIRTEEN

Four years went by. It seemed that history repeated itself. One visiting day in July, hot and sticky weather, Caroline all red and sweaty, said to John that she can not wait for him any longer and she met a good man that offered her marriage and was willing to adopt the twins.

John felt very empty. He lost his wife and children and now he was going to lose his mistress and his children. Once again John said nothing. But the news hit John heavily.

For the next few days he couldn't function.

He was devastated and depressed and very sad. The warden watched John and after a few days John was sent to the counsellor office for therapy.

John did not trust therapists. He had bad experiences in his childhood with them and felt they put words in his mouth. As a child all he wanted was his mother and the therapist always criticised his mother in front of him and told him how bad person and mother she was. As a child he was angry with the therapist all the time and now in prison as a man he was sent yet again to a session with a therapist.

He just set there starring at the counsellor saying nothing for forty five minutes.

After three sessions John was acquitted for seeing a counsellor. It took John a while to adjust to the idea of losing Caroline and the twins too which he never saw for fifteen years.

He concentrated on his work and studies. He sat the final exams in constructing building engineering in Jail. John was all exited, waiting for two weeks for the results. He couldn't sleep or eat properly.

At last the day arrived. The guard came to his cell in mid afternoon and said:

"John I have an envelope for you". John was busy working on some greeting cards. He looked at the guard, got up from his chair, stared at the hands holding the big brown envelope. The guard gave him the envelope and waited. He also wanted to know the results. John finally managed to open the envelope with shake hands.

A shiny certificate with a covering letter was inside. John read the letter with a shaky voice: "Congratulation, we are pleased to inform you.....you made the Fourteenth place in all Britain, in the 'City and Guilds' qualification. John stared at the certificate, it had two sides to it. The achievement of City and Guilds 'clerk of the works' in building construction, and the other side of the certificate stated 'Drain's engineer'.

The guard was so excited from John achievements that he started shouting, "He got it, he got it, well done".

All the inmates that were at the time in their cells run towards John's cell to congratulate him.

John was so happy and in a very long time he shade a tear. He knew in his heart that things would change for him for the better. He promised himself to use this event to better his life and be a better human been.

CHAPTER FOURTEEN

Six month later, in the springtime, in a bright sunny glorious morning, John was released.

He made his way home. When he arrived he saw his wife Bridget at home.

The children were at their in law's as usual. Bridget was happy to see him again.

All the talks about divorcing him while he was in prison were forgotten. John promised her that he will go straight and he will work harder for his family.

John did not realise the problems he would face find a job as an ex-con. The entire neighbourhood where he lived knew about his time in prison, and they stigmatised him.

Weeks went by and John couldn't find any work. He spent most of his time in the local pub with his friends. His relationship with Bridget worsens.

John offered her to move to another area where people don't know them and start from the beginning. Bridget did not want to move anywhere.

She was comfortable with her in law's looking after the children.

It was a summer time. One hot day in August, John moved to the next town searching for work. John walked in the local pub in Colchester ordering himself a beer.

He was talking to the barman about work, making inquires about the builders in the area.

A local elderly farmer was sitting in a corner table drinking his beer, he couldn't avoid hearing John talking about construction and building work. The farmer approached John and said: "Can I talk to you over a drink". John looked at the farmer and moved to sit in his table. The farmer offered John a job as a decorator and fixer for his four double old cottages near by . In return for John's work the farmer said: "I'll give you a basic salary and when you finish the works I will give you a cottage with a two Acers of land, and you can be a farmer, and while you work on my cottages you can live in one of them".

John was excited about the idea of being a farmer. He always liked animals and nature. John work hard on the cottages, cleaning, painting, fixing wooden windows and tried very hard to restore the old glory looking of the cottages. John worked from early mornings to late evenings in an effort to finish the job.

Six months he worked very hard, did not spent money in the pub like all his local friends, and managed to keep himself and support his family by sending them money every week on a regular basis.

After he finished his job, the farmer kept his promise and gave him a cottage with two Acres land. John wanted to start farming. But to be able to purchase live stock, he needed some capital. So he had to continue working as a decorator and carpenter in the local area and save his wages as much as he could, for one whole year he did not go out spending money and worked anywhere he could in the building trade. After almost a year of hard work, he managed to buy fifty chickens and two big Labrador dogs.

For a couple of years he worked on his farm. He developed his farming skills.

He was a quick learner and he loved exploring new fields and gain knowledge.

He sold the chicken's eggs to the local shops, and grew vegetables in his farm for his consumption and for commercial prophases. He managed to make a living from his farm.

After a while John heard that the scrapyardman that pointed at him as a gang leader was shot on his both knees. John was wondering who did it? He also thought this is his punishment for daubing to the police, which result for John to lose five years of his life in prison.

CHAPTER FIFTEEN

He made a lot of new friends from all walks of life. He had police men friends, army soldiers from a near by army base, builders and engineers.

He through parties at his farm for his friends, and they were drinking and smoking, dancing and laughing to the music of the 'Beetles' and 'Rock and Roll' until the small hours of the morning. Some of the lads had used to go straight to work and some of them just crushed anywhere in John's cottage floor and slept until late afternoon.

John's parties had a wide reputation in the all area. One morning after a wild party John woke up in the arms of a blond woman. He lit a cigarette and than rubbed his eyes and looked at her sleeping beside him with her arm around him, he moved her arm gently, She woke up. "Who are you"? John asked her. He couldn't remember how she got in his bed. "I am Lucy", she said. "What's the time" she asked, and John said "eleven o'clock", "Oh my God, I am late for work". She said and jumped off put her cloths on and disappeared.

John was gob smacked. After a little while he got up and sorts himself. He barley could walk around the cottage. His friends where sleeping on the floor everywhere. He left the cottage to the field to do his chores, feeding his chickens and his dogs and attended to his vegetable field.

Late afternoon his friends started leaving to their homes.

He was invited too, to their parties in the police force and the army base. John had good times than. He worked in his farm and managed a good living. He also had fun being popular among his friends.

John continued to support his family financially, but he rarely visited his family and his visits grew apart and far between.

Five happy years went by and one sunny day in June, the local council approached him and offered him to perches his farm land. They explained John that the land is needed to build a primary school.

John considered the offer. Weighting it in his mind. "What to do?" This was a great opportunity to full fill his dream to go to London.

That night he went to see his family and to try and discus it with Bridget.

When he walked in the door the children were playing, they looked at him barley recognising their father. Prior to this visit John was there four   months before.

The children ran to their mother asking who is this man. "Your father" she said in a resentment voice, and now "Go to bed, I come very soon to tuck you in".

John was standing in the living room watching his children. He was very sad that they did not remember him. He decided there and than to come more often to see them.

When the children were sort out. Bridget offered John some coffee.

She said to him: "What brought you here tonight". John explained Bridget about the council's offer on his farm land and about his dream to move to London.

He also explained Bridget that this is a good opportunity to a new start all over again as a family.

Bridget was very quiet, listening to him, and than she said: "If you are thinking about moving to London, I want a divorce, in no circumstances I am moving with my children to London". "Why not" asked John. "It is to far away from my parents in Law" she said. She could not even think of leaving them behind.

She was so used to it, them helping her with the children.

John was very quiet tried to think and than he said: "O.k. we get a divorce, I will pay you sum lamp of money for the children's keep and you give me visiting rights to come and see them".

Bridget reply straight away and said: "Yes, a good idea".

The divorce procedures took a couple of weeks. At that time John got his money from the council, a substantial sum. He kept his promise and paid Bridget the agreed amount for his children's keep.

John sort himself out. Selling his possessions, like some furniture he had in his cottage. It took him three weeks to finish his business in Colchester. Including some building work he done for some clients.

He gather some new phone numbers and addresses in London which his friends provided him with, so he can start rebuild his life again.

He felt so free and excited of moving to London.

He couldn't wait to fulfil his dream.

A day before his moving to London, in the evening he went to see his children. This time they greeted him with joy, remembering their father.

The four little girls, and the two little boys ranging from four years old to twelve years old jumped on him, kissing and cuddling him. They all asked him: "can we come with you daddy?". John was overwhelmed from his children's affections and reactions. He said: " you stay with your mother, and look after her for me, and I promise to come and visit you when I am settle in London. I also will take you with me to London on weekends from time to time". The children looked disappointed, they wanted to go with their father there and than.

Bridget called out for them, "It is bed time children, tomorrow you have school".The children tried hard to protest and stay a bit longer with him, until John said to his children: "Listen to your mother, I come and tuck you in". The children kissed their father and went to bed. John finished his coffee with Bridget and went and tuck his children in their bed, kissing them.

Tears were streaming on his face when he left, he knew in his heart that it will take a while until he will be able to see his children again.

He went back to his cottage, the place was empty, it was late at night about eleven o'clock, he felt an urge to leave straight away. He took his pack bag with a few of his cloths, had a quick last look at his farm, remembering the good times he had the past five years and left making his way to the train station, destination Waterloo – London.